# DESERT DECAY

Desert Decay

Published by Gatekeeper Press
2167 Stringtown Rd, Suite 109
Columbus, OH 43123-2989
www.GatekeeperPress.com

Library of Congress Control Number: 2022933981

ISBN (hardcover): 9781662925078
ISBN (paperback): 9781662925085
eISBN: 9781662925092

# DESERT DECAY

*poems* ANNA CARRANZA

Columbus, Ohio

# Part I

Meet Me at The Corner of The Next Dream ............... 1
Lost in Mango Juice ....................................... 2
Ombré Effect .............................................. 3
Colony Hotel .............................................. 4
Moonshot ................................................. 5
Newport Noir ............................................. 6
Baby, I'm On It ........................................... 7
Cherry Meltdown ......................................... 8
Afternoon Sun ............................................ 9
Churning ................................................. 10
Jawn ..................................................... 11
Spring Break ............................................. 12
Desert Decay ............................................. 13
Cannon Ball .............................................. 14
Maybe We Should Stay Another Day ................... 15
Room 38 ................................................. 16
Lazy Sundays ............................................ 17
Good Hospitality ........................................ 18
South Swell .............................................. 19
Curveball ................................................ 20
Night Is Young ........................................... 21
Enigmatic Blonde ....................................... 22
Dirty Pool ............................................... 23
Planet Venus ............................................. 24
Since We Did It .......................................... 25
Sound Bath .............................................. 26
Pool Astronaut .......................................... 27

# Part II

Shark Bait ........................................................ 31
Doris ............................................................. 32
Shimmer .......................................................... 33
A Heart-Shaped Bathtub ........................................... 34
Etiquette ........................................................ 35
Enchanted ........................................................ 36
Think Highbrow ................................................... 37
Beloved .......................................................... 38
Little One ....................................................... 39
Mars Adjacent .................................................... 40
Interlude ........................................................ 41
Blurred Innocence ................................................ 42
A Dash of Salt ................................................... 43
Cicada Season .................................................... 44
I Fool Around with A Porsche or Maserati Occasionally ............ 45
Destiny Inn ...................................................... 46
Close It with Crescendo .......................................... 47
Frozen Raw Steak ................................................. 48
Pale Rabbit Hole ................................................. 49
No Vacancy ....................................................... 50
By The Bird Rock ................................................. 51
Fatal Misadventures .............................................. 52
Common Language .................................................. 53
Lavish Anonymity ................................................. 54
Down In the Deep ................................................. 55
Sage ............................................................. 56

# Part III

The Stars Are Not Done with Me ............................... 61
The Dead Deer on the Ride Back .............................. 62
Douse Your Table with Excellence ........................... 63
Rain As an Aphrodisiac ............................................. 64
Sentimental Stubbornness ....................................... 65
Final Entrée ................................................................ 66
Outskirts of Town ..................................................... 67
I PM ............................................................................ 68
Hawaiian Blend ......................................................... 69
Plot Twist ................................................................... 70
Trophies ..................................................................... 71
Let Us Traverse in Reverse ....................................... 72
Ball at Midcourt ........................................................ 73
Cadence in Autumn .................................................. 74
Next Stop: Oceanside ............................................... 75
Nocturnal Tendencies .............................................. 76
QT With the Pup ........................................................ 77
Stay Gold Chico ......................................................... 79
Surfliner ..................................................................... 80
Sweet Science ............................................................ 81
Viejo Bridge ............................................................... 82

*In memory of Chico*

"It was good to be in California....
You couldn't feel safe anywhere, except the desert..."

—Henry Miller, *The Air-Conditioned Nightmare*

# Part I

# Meet Me at the Corner of the Next Dream

Partially cloudy on a Tuesday
 at sixty-three degrees.
There was a dry heat
that compressed
us like pancakes.
Simply giving into the curves
of the motion as
we sipped iced
 coffee with paper straws.
 The last train departing
business class specific.
 We wrapped
our arms
 around things unsettled.
 Optimistic
hoping for a nice sunset.

# Lost in Mango Juice

私はあなたの腕の中にいて、
　　　　　あなたは私を舐めている
あなたはオッズを信じることができますか?

# Ombré Effect

The sun poured like a
  glass of lemonade
on the Moroccan hard tile.
  White-hot and mundane
  we were high up.

# Colony Hotel

It would be about noon when
 she wanted to get in her early swims.
Checked her reflection in the wishbone mirror.
She slung her denim beach bag over her shoulder.
Briskly skipped down the white stone steps.
She noticed the silver tray
 scattered with yesterday's dining.
Balmy dry weather and overwhelming
smell of gardenias.
*It's all I ever wanted,*
she told herself until numb with conviction.

# Moonshot

Dear girl from nowhere,
 Oh, you are such
 a gorgeous mystery!
I think you want an adventure.
 Burn your thoughts.
 Long afternoons
involving ice cream and waffles.
Have
 you been
to pig island?
They are like pigeons.
Bigger, with mouths and teeth.
 Whenever, let me know.
Find a place
 for you to go.

# Newport Noir

This is a love story
 I apologize
in advance
no refunds.

# Baby, I'm On It

The waiter nodded, assuring her water would be chilled
with a slice of fresh lemon.
Comforting. They got off on a rough start
*Forget the small stuff.*
*The moment when the arguments get redundant.*
Eager Nora spoke about fairy tales.
Desperate little things.
Trying to control love.
She arrived with a bag of fancy clothes.
Terrifically stunning and prepared
for a languid stay.
Like a rip curl in July
her smile was easy to provoke.

# Cherry Meltdown

Counting down the minutes
when I can make you laugh
in that way.
When we were
happy with the idea of us and
the sparkling sea.
We dared to jump in the darkest
 of nights fueled
on baklava and rum.
How tedious it must
be when we can't be free.

# Afternoon Sun

A man in a tattered straw hat
   white hair wet
closes his eyes to the sea.
Quickly hums a familiar song.
A canvas of memories.
Brushes his octaves
    \_\_\_\_\_ acoustics heard on the reef at Cress Street
shaping the mood farther south.

# Churning

Into the night we drove.
Remember when we first took
that trip to find each other?
 It was then our lives marbleized.
Shaped by extreme precarity, eventually the
roads lead to us.
I worry about you, your insomnia.
 those thoughts
 you have when the rest are still.
Please get some more coffee,
this will be a long ride,
 my sweet dove.

# Jawn

There is nothing like *jawn*
Tell me.
What other word?
An all-purpose word.
Repeat it slowly. Let it roll off your tongue.
When a fellow says jawn it could be like ...
Man, look at that fine ass lady Ricky brought back from the party!
She *jawn*--
Or, that steak was *jawn*
Man, this hurts like *jawn*
Put some green pepper on that *jawn*
It's a word like no other.
You can
sprinkle it
  on anything.

# Spring Break

Driving down the sultry coast
glimpses of the sunset
just heaven
crème de la crème
can't stop craving this.

# Desert Decay

We had a gypsy lifestyle,
going from
 hotel to hotel.
So, we are all travelers now. In it together.
How about we stay here and dream for a while?
Before our desert utopia becomes ripe for fraud.

# Cannon Ball

Well executed, the mighty red-haired boy
hurled chlorine and coconut oil
from the sky
tsunami splash ...
 Copious amounts.
No one was dry.

# Maybe We Should Stay Another Day

This is a good place for us.
Why go back so soon?
He brushes a fallen eyelash off her cheek.
A bluish haze from
the television screen makes them
glow in the dark room.

She sees his tattoo of a tree.
Left of his lower spine. It curves
to the back area up to the shoulder.
Where the branches
extend to the side of his ribs.
Love to see that. She imagines the tattoo
of a tiger she longs for. The problem is
finding the right one. It's hard. Originality.
When she sees it, she will know.

# Room 38

I spread out my sunburned skin
 Like a starfish against
the cool crisp linen until it
 became a snow angel
Bilal walked
out, already in his board shorts

how miniscule we must look from outer space

# Lazy Sundays

Did you bring the goods?
She smiled, revealing a half-tattered book of crossword puzzles.
I can't
figure this out.
I think I'm getting dumber at a much faster rate.
Sneak in your favorite word
at 75-down.
Note your initials.
Top?
That's a bold choice.
How long could she carry on with this charade?
I'm still trying to figure
 out who Garfield's girlfriend is.
Arlene. Duh.

# Good Hospitality

Carte blanche immunity runs amuck.
Magical. Spanish Colonial
Wrought iron gates,
gusts of dusty wind
and blood feuds.
A love story with
tragic ribboned consequences, and
great service.

# South Swell

You're not from this earth
 but please stay on my account.
 I look at your eyes
  damp and ready
for a high-speed chase.
Streetlights and emerald spilled
 it's only noon.

# Curveball

Bring us something delicious if we are to
 survive this.
Certainly, a bottle of gin.
With her usual glamourous shrug and
halfcocked grin
the phone began to ring.
Torrid heat swirls on the glass
drifted into a rush of sex.

# Night Is Young

Shot clock turned respectably.
Welcome back.
Light is pinkish bright.
Lead by example
devil nods
Timing is everything,
champagne awaits.

# Enigmatic Blonde

the maid/left the door slightly
open/vintage mid-century coffee table
bamboo wallpaper/beige stilettos
the morning dragged on/she was surly
sure of her certainty
looked tremendous/lock + loaded
her white hair shimmied down
her waist/ alabaster skin
took small drags
of a skinny cigarette
like her name was Lana
coiled like
 a serpent/in another
life she was a dancer.

# Dirty Pool

When you all aren't looking
pink flamingo goes to work.
Keep the kiddies safely entertained.
Baby skin
whimsical fodder
deflated by the end of the day.
Crickets find a place to play.

# Planet Venus

Fortress in the granite soil
exotic company.
 Bleached bones
long hot nights and sexy pools.
Peach fuzz and Gucci shoes.
No more second thoughts.
With new eyes, in the gingham bikini
He could see me looking rotten.
*I love it here with you*
Slowly we stopped talking about other things.

# Since We Did It

Like lavender petals,
it pours over me.
Like sweet yakitori.
My life in diamonds.
I saw the girls as specks and
free-floating shapes as my eyelids
grew heavier.
Lips and long limbs.
Washes of color.
Red.
They became faceless.
Beautiful little creatures.
Sensory afterglow.

# Sound Bath

Musical tools cluttered the floor like condiments
strewn out randomly, his fingers moved fast
Carefully, he sorted out the variety
of percussion instruments, crystal singing bowls, gongs,
and his precious pan drum.
Each one laid with precision.
The bones of it, crisp clean lines.
Closed each instrument
with delicate custody.

# Pool Astronaut

The sun has gone to bed.
Heaven is not far away
    star walkers with webbed feet
delve into the deep end of the Milky Way
intergalactic nebula
 condensed in their memories
  weightless
 purging the dark water.

# Part II

# Shark Bait

Left side of kidney bean pool
strangers
share a cigarette. The girl
presses her palm over her lips
she wants her pound of flesh.

# Doris

Rather pale complexion, somewhat
 of an appalling snob.
Adds to the Moroccan tapestry.
Hovers around the property
like a spectral nightclub  singer.
 Self-appointed status purveyor.
Her previous incarnation.
Once desirable in that effortless manner,
she fell madly in love with a deviant art dealer
and that added to her fable.
A macabre series of misfortunate events.
Rumors swirl around the stucco cottage where the petunias
grow wild, some say
he is buried there.
She is not afraid of what happens in the dark.

# Shimmer

Can I have a taste of that?
There was a silver lining to the revelry.
A space where the moon could not presume its promise.
We saw a sliver of an exit to this mad world. I had to decide
and chose to delve into the shimmer.
Forget whatever
was left behind.

# A Heart-Shaped Bathtub

Inside the bubble tower
Nestled in the oversized porcelain cocoon
there was a glamorous house,
where I pray
for most of the afternoon.
Candles on the gilded vanity
flickering lights chatter in morse code,
musky mold that reek of jasmine and wild ideas.

# Etiquette

*Oh no, love! We never eat.*
*The heat about dries up everything.*
*You will lose your cravings.*
*We all do.*

# Enchanted

Screaming children
race into the haunted glow.
We walked without direction into purple forests.
Trees can talk.
Breathing shadows showed us the way.
Focus on the dancing ghosts' reflections in the lake,
Which unfortunately made me lose my phone in the black wat
I chased it until the rocks made my knees bleed.

# Think Highbrow

Buckle up, buttercup
the best is yet to come, my cherry pop.
Imagine if we took back the
good shape of our hearts, thoughts
in this dim light, the love story remains.
One day
we will get back
to our lives.

# Beloved

How do I know tonight will be full of merriment?
The buttery roll seemed to melt in his mouth.
Lingering, I caught some running down the side
near his dimple with my tongue.
Taste of peppermint and sweat.
Soft rain parlayed with bluegrass music promised
luxurious unwrapped gifts
saved for tomorrow morning.

# Little One

The neon highway behind us.
Let's go for more. Figure it out as we go.
 Strange real moments.
They pop and crackle.
Our skin slipped into delicious knots.
Under the leisurely water's flow, we go.
  We swam to the inner cove.
Salty wind whipping our hair. Nourishing old scars.
Everyone believes we are up to no good.
Perhaps.
We would counter and
 define good?
There is no way back.
We moved slower until we were on the far side of the beach
and could
 no longer see shattered glass.

# Mars Adjacent

Sometimes you must go from
acidic bitters to candied honey.
Days blurred into sweet tar,
each one more euphoric and
stranger than the one before.
I saw a grasshopper for the first
time in a while.
Where the heck did it come from?
And why was it gone for so long?

# Interlude

*You smell like peaches,* he blurted out.
She caught his worried resting face in the microwave oven's reflection.
That's about it
*You smell like peaches.*

# Blurred Innocence

*The road is so steep*
*and the ocean calls me to*
 *stop and static hits the radio*
*into ......*

# A Dash of Salt

I lay with my love. He sends me promises of a motionless kiss.
There we would find a silence to the challenging matters
of obstructions.
Which I craved in these dark days. I can't remember a
moment when it was organic.
Like the eggs. Hardboiled and a dash of salt.
It would be so much better if dairy didn't make me sad
Ergo, I can't develop a craving for cheese.
It would affect my palette in an unfortunate way.
Then it could be an easier way to find an exit strategy,
I would imagine.
I've been taking the wrong ones.
I only pray that this world can offer me up to you.
Because I can't remember the kiss right now.
Nothing about this is right.
Like cheese
something I can do without.

# Cicada Season

August held an extraordinary
canvas for brevity.
Still, it seemed desert summers went on forever.
The vigor hiss of the cicadas
telling the time of day.
Horny little bugs
fervently mating.
Buzzing the trees dry.

# I Fool Around with a Porsche or Maserati Occasionally

What is your ideology? I took
 a long sip and stared at
the amplified memory
tacked on the wall.
Remarkably the afternoon
coffee was still warm.
Always so callous,
those empty promises.
Grandstanding can get you places.

# Destiny Inn

He fancied himself a desert heathen
the sycophants
kneeling before him.
All the exits closed.
 In the hot wind,
he would get a sense of them
until
they all lost track
of time.

# Close It with Crescendo

Starting game with
a kickstart.
Run it forward
Maximum casualties.
No shortcuts.

# Frozen Raw Steak

While alone with her thoughts,
the speed of motion
gave her a migraine.
Juices lingered before overflowing the plate.
The meat pulsated,
 squirmed around.
This wine is something else.
Pushed into her head and formed hallucinations.
Slim and mercurial,
complicit they were.
He was often smiling.
The thought of him watching caused
endless tingles
along her crooked spine.

# Pale Rabbit Hole

We looked away knowing.
He waited for the valet to come.
Affluence rules.
No, he would not have a less wasted life.
He turned to speak and could not
It seemed important.
I hurried
into the safety
of the car.
His pain obvious.
We were no longer
curious talking to strangers.

## No Vacancy

The elusive exit to the other side
led the women to
believe something else was at play.
 *Do you ever think about leaving?*
Defiant they wait for the
sound of their lovers' knock at the front door.

# By The Bird Rock

Slip of a woman.
Slender and not very tall.
Skin peeled too soon.
No towels to dry.
No longer her skin.
Never cared for flesh.
Water puddles near her bare feet.
Pale moonlight she went to lay down with her man.

# Fatal Misadventures

When she was asleep, he spoke softly
 into her ear, *adore you*
The next day,
 he was left alone
and decided to go on a night swim.
Find new prey.
His tactics were changing.

# Common Language

She had a moment to relax at the pool
 before checkout.
There remained a beautiful trace
of people subtly conversating
without divide. The heat
rousing all inhibitions. They had
grown more magnificent and
idle with their distaste for the real world.
Flirting under the white and blue umbrellas.
Effectively creating a colony laid out
with olives and ginger tonics.

# Lavish Anonymity

I have cinematic dreams,
randoms and famous people
 and situations that I don't normally
think about. Food porn,
 I dream about
 mango et
 dulce de leche
a lot.

# Down In The Deep

I want to hover above the San Joaquin Mountains.
The lizards will dance with no music.
At the crest, my family will blow kisses and
send up red balloons.
Hot tears will fall like raindrops on them
as they dance like
adorable goblins.
My auntie will greet me,
 she is no longer comatose.
Sleep and dust from her stale breath will
be released
*I've been coming here for years, dear heart.*

# Sage

Those white elephants.
Everything else remained thick, gray, and invisible.
The water was considerably more, vast, and exposed
when viewed from this height.
He grinned at the panoramic ocean view.
 A white fedora hat with the brim down.
Ebony skin looked like fine
 dark chocolate pressed
 against linen white
 guayabera shirt and trousers.

# Part III

# The Stars Are Not Done with Me

The Ford F-150  is humming
 outside like a champ,
fully loaded bells and whistles.
Thoughts
 like wildfire,
spreading expeditiously.
Smile for me. I don't want
to be captured.

# The Dead Deer on the Ride Back

It didn't look too dead. It had its sheen and remained
an incredibly
beautiful animal still.
I drove two miles later sobbing quite terribly.
I must say, overwhelmed.
The red light to Country Club Drive is forever long.
A fun song came on and I got nauseous.
Who hit that deer and what did they feel?
I wanted to go back.
Get in front of the other cars that could possibly run over
its carcass. Perhaps, there was some reminder of its spirit and
it needed me to help its passage to wherever it was heading out
that fateful morning.
I wanted to put my hands up and fervently jump up and down
until
more help would come. Wrap myself around it. Until it felt safe.
The beautiful beast would be at peace somehow.
My knuckles clutched the wheel.
But I didn't.
Instead, it went into my gut.
I cried even more undetermined.
Praying for the damn light to turn green.

# Douse Your Table with Excellence

Everything goes when you go down a buffet line.
Like I said. It all goes together.
I love raw vegetables. I can't taste it.
The women in my family have a deep love with the kitchen.
They brush and prepare food with tears and spices.
Next time, I know to check my appliances
 and make sure they work.
My guests are so forgiving.
They say thank you to everyone.

# Rain As an Aphrodisiac

Spitting.
 Drizzling. Splattering.
Heavy shredding and cold to the core.
 Give us more. So, we can feel it in our liver
Our groins cry for us to
 surrender and dance in it.
Tongues stuck out
hoping it would saturate the heat.
Distilled and seething.
Soaked it up clean.

# Sentimental Stubbornness

Nourishing old scars
if we keep them out, it
destroys them; if we let them in, it destroys us.
 We don't seem to understand
obvious things that are
staring us in the
 face.

# Final Entrée

Take care to chop the cilantro properly,
promise me.
Also, that we will
not be drowning in debt.
How sensitive you are to cutting onions
tears will get into broth. Which will
only make me cry eating it.
Remember joy instead, eliminate details.
Petty fights.

# Outskirts of Town

Exhausted and loosened
Thrown off the trail.
Less than a third of a tank left.
The alternative was to slam the brakes.
Ten minutes later
the fireflies led to an unseen path.
Resolve comes in many forms.

# 1 pm

Cue
the
rain.

# Hawaiian Blend

The secret to my baby's
layered cake is
island splendor. Summers make him
slightly sinister.
Toward treacherous resistance
I keep him spinning. Unfurling
our curiosities.
We shower together in the
middle of the night.
He has spiritual journeys that include me.
Once upon a time we were strangers
 on this planet seeking a home.
He is my refuge.
I would like to wish him a
happy birthday for the
next half a century or so.

# Plot Twist

I don't
want to
know
I don't want to know
its only inevitable, I will at some
point
know

# Trophies

Off with your head.
Now you are dead.
I circumvent your morality for some more sensuality.
I cannot hear you now.
Our plans exceed this common ground.
I cannot think of a more tragic affair.
Suddenly
all hell breaks loose.
When the dust finally settles, I am gone
and you are stuck
without a noose.

# Let Us Traverse in Reverse

Rosé saturated play dates
frosty sprinkled cupcakes make for fantastic
housewarming gifts.
Delicate indecisions.
*Drink more water.*
Where is everyone summering?
Who is the best realtor in the desert?
Just the good parts.
Husbands and nanny problems.
Beautifully crafted floral setting.
Candy cane straws pairs well with the
glitter sweet lip gloss
as they sip arsenic tonics
 mixed with gossip.
What to do with all that free time?

# Ball at Midcourt

Game night.
 They came from an illustrious line of accomplished
athletic enthusiasts.
*Bobby Hurley. Oh man. What a game. That kid is talented as the sun
is hot.*
Her father bonding over sports, college basketball to be precise
Duke beating Kentucky in overtime by a point. How about that?
 *Greatest college game ever played in my humble opinion.*
The husband had all his teams make the final four. Duke,
Michigan, Cincinnati, Indiana. It felt like he was back on script.
The bookies were answering his calls again. That put him back
in the circle.
That one shot almost made my heart stop man. Christian
Laettner's game winning iconic shot.
*They can't put that genie back into the bottle that's for sure.*
The husband nicknamed her Golden Child.
She had a knack for picking the winning teams simply from not
knowing anything about the game or players.
 Before that she liked to watch figure skating and that's about it.
The tournament's arrival of
 Michigan's infamous Fab Five changed all that. Chris Webber,
Jalen Rose, Juwan Howard, Jimmy King, and Ray Jackson.
The Wolverines delivered excitement.
Resorted to yelling at a tv monitor, after the bookies cut him off.
That seemed like lifetimes ago

# Cadence in Autumn

I don't think it is soft.
The scarf.
It wasn't uncomfortable.
But at a further glance.
I found it to be quite irksome.
It showed the bitter patterns of matter that held
 me too close to a memory.
Despite the differences, it found itself back to me.
Occasionally, I decided it would be of value again.
Then it happened.
The feeling of rain.
Pointed itself right back at me.
What I failed to understand: why I lost it in the first place.
Outside of the eclipse, there were hints.
They only said things in dreams.
In silence things said, popped up in illusions.
I was calmed by these shifts.
The answers came and went.
The scarf scratched my back.
It was not so much that I allowed its digs
One day it would be on different flesh, and the
 smell of me would be theirs.

# Next Stop: Oceanside

Last call for Irvine Station.
She struggles with her messy bun.
Her dry chapped lips bother her.
Rather than search for the
small tube of moisturizer,
she picks at it.
Her thoughts consumed by the desert.
Closing doors. Loop of hillsides
 with lime green patches.

# Nocturnal Tendencies

She never mentioned those late-night walks.
Her leather backpack clung
so tight it would
leave marks on her back
in the morning.
Dried up by cacti
and the
occasional tumbleweed.

# QT With The Pup

We saw a dead bird today.
Two birds to be honest.
The added irony to this was
I had the dream two nights ago.
A bird dead as could be
lay facing up.
Its white carcass presented itself to the sky.
Decapitated. I found my dog to
be hiding something
in his mouth.
This became a tug of war.
Each of us determined. We scuffled.
And I think
he gave into me while we were
amid this entanglement.
Discovering we are not who we think we are.
He thought it through perhaps.
The way he relinquished
his predatory nature.
I have not seen this side of my dog.
He is still a puppy.
Sometimes I wonder if he is the spawn
of unnatural beasts but that is
yet
to tell itself.
I won eventually.
I suppose.

If this is considered a win, I guess.
My dog held the head of the bird in his mouth.
Mind you this was his second visit to the beach.
Sometimes he thinks about the bird.
I know he does.
 I wonder what his next target will be.
 It's okay.
The summer is still young.

# Stay Gold Chico

From behind lavender clouds
 undone
by the violent sea.
Did we win yet? For a moment,
 you were seen past the swells
like so many brilliant memories
 inside a broken pearl.

# Surfliner

*Trains are so romantic, shame on anyone who doesn't*
*appreciate the true beauty of the machine.*
*Locomotives are the best way to see the country,*
said the woman with a nuanced Southern accent
and a lazy left eye.
The moisture on the glass made it hard to see outside.
We were like a caterpillar
winding deep in the earth.

# Sweet Science

A reminder if I had married you
that day
when we ran around
devouring the world
I would have worn
 a black dress that
 would not bleed through
 The fit perfect,
obviously.
Lovely to slip into
sheer
flawless.
Until an embroidery got caught
 on my wrist and pricked my skin
 the small dots
that formed evenly.

# Viejo Bridge

The penny taste of
 blood filled her mouth.
She preferred the sudden movements of the sea
when one couldn't hear anything
else but
the reckless ache of waves.
Pure air.
Thin sharpness inside
her ears cut through
the skull like a tungsten knife.
She forged
ahead.